THE DOOR
STANDING OPEN

*for Joe Gabriel
with warm regards*

Robert Mezey

November 1984

ROBERT MEZEY

THE DOOR STANDING OPEN

New and Selected Poems

LONDON
OXFORD UNIVERSITY PRESS
MELBOURNE TORONTO
1970

Oxford University Press, Ely House, London W. 1

GLASGOW NEW YORK TORONTO MELBOURNE WELLINGTON
CAPE TOWN SALISBURY IBADAN NAIROBI DAR ES SALAAM LUSAKA ADDIS ABABA
BOMBAY CALCUTTA MADRAS KARACHI LAHORE DACCA
KUALA LUMPUR SINGAPORE HONG KONG TOKYO

SBN 19 211288 0

© Oxford University Press 1970

*Printed in Great Britain by
The Bowering Press Plymouth*

FOR

BILL & GLORIA & RUSS & ANN

All that I have—
Handfuls of wind,
A gift for the kingdom of birds.

FOREWORD

The five poems I have called, half-seriously, 'someone else's poems' are from a book written almost fifteen years ago. Looking through it for something to include in this selection, I found I could hardly bear to read most of the poems, they were so full of the deadly and slavish atmosphere in which I first began to write poetry. At last I ended with five poems in which a real voice and real feelings had survived, though almost drowned in the verbiage and pretense of that period, and took the liberty of rewriting them thoroughly, a work that I tried to do in the spirit of a man restoring an old canvas.

I have included the Greenberg poems because they are in some way closer to me than most of my own poems, and because they embody the swiftness and simplicity I aim for. They are true collaborations, and I must thank Ben Zion Gold, who taught me to understand and to hear.

For the Ady poem I am deeply indebted to the Hungarian poet Francisco Kalnay, who gave me a version not far from the final one.

Finally I want to thank the many students and teachers who, after I was fired from Fresno State College for speaking truth to power, helped to sustain me through the past year, during which most of the new poems were written.

ACKNOWLEDGMENTS

Acknowledgments are due to the editors of the following magazines in which some of these poems first appeared: *Backwash, Botteghe Oscure, Harper's, kayak, Liberation, New Orleans Poetry Journal, New Yorker, Paris Review, Poetry, Stand, Transpacific,* and *Unicorn Folio.*

Also to The Cummington Press, which originally published the poems in the first two sections, as well as 'Last Words'.

Also to the Three People Press, which first published *The Mercy of Sorrow.*

CONTENTS

The Mercy of Sorrow

The Door Standing Open

Neither descendant nor lucky ancestor,
neither relative nor acquaintance,
I am of no one.
I am of no one.
I am, as every man, nobility,
North Pole, mystery, strangeness
and a distant light,
a distant light.

But oh God, I can't take it any more!
I would like to reveal myself
so that you may see me,
so that you may know me.
For this, everything—
self torture, song—
I would love to be loved and to belong to someone,
and to belong to someone.

after Ady

Someone Else's Poems

The Funeral Home

In the environs of the funeral home
The smell of death was absent. All there was
Was flowers rioting, the odors blown
Palpable as a blossom into the face,
To be crushed and overpower—as if the grass
Already covered the nostrils in that place.

Hyacinths, larkspur, irises, flags of summer
Beating the air morning and evening to metal
Immortality, or opening to a bee's clamor
The delicate parts, warm and smelling faintly
Of wine, already dying, the damp petal
Swaying a little with the weight of the bee's body—

Let them cut these flowers. Let them be ruddy
And golden and white and let them be
Heaped up and overflowing over the body
Waiting to be put down. To be unborn.
Something is sprouting in dark mahogany
Out of them—edged, and shining like a thorn.

Sky Full of Dead

After the noise and spasm of battle, a lull
Invaded the thinned camp, and all the soldiers,
Turning their blackened faces to the sky
And the small hills they had held, that held their dead,
Lay down with the guns that bartered lives for lives.
The sun was down and the hills were cold and blue.

The sun went down and the hills got cold and blue
Only after battle. The usual lull
Was an endless noon haze when they wielded their lives
Against the grain of boredom. The toil of soldiers
Stiffened their hands and clothes. There were few dead,
And even a sniper's fire became the sky.

They almost hungered for battle. The daily sky
Was their true enemy, dressed in shimmering blue,
A smiling magician who could transform the dead
Or make a dream come true in the hot lull—
Lullabye, hallucination, blood-spurting soldier!
His images loosened the foothold of their lives.

Invisible, then not, dead, then alive
And breathing on your bread, the old sky
Turns you against your will, to become soldiers
Running beneath a sky almost as blue
And brilliant as it was in the ideal lull
Of childhood, when no one could be dead.

Now past the hammocks swinging with the dead,
You hunt among the blasted trees for the lives
You have never led, for the spasms that can lull
Bare nerves to sleep, that can eclipse the sky—
And perhaps when you wake, you will find it blue
And the air cold, and yourselves, no longer soldiers.

Others may hope to make peace. You are soldiers.
At night you can see the half-naked dead
Bodies turning to mud, shining blue

4

Under the moon, and all you have is your lives
And your blood struggling and beating under the sky.
Star-rise, moon-rise, only another lull.

Shadows of tall soldiers rise in the sky
In the midnight lull. They shoulder their heavy lives.
They are blue hills carrying many dead.

To Levine on the Day of Atonement

Impenitent, we meet again,
As Gentile as your wife or mine,
And pour into a jelly glass
The cheapest California wine.

Jewless in Gaza, we have come
Where worldly likenesses commence
Gathering fury, and still we keep
Some dark, essential difference.

Is it the large half-chiseled nose,
That monument to daily breath?
Is it some fiber in the heart
That makes the heart believe in death?

God only knows. And who is he?
That cold comedian of our harm.
I wear its red stains on my sleeve,
You like a scar on either arm,

But neither knows what good it does.
The voiceless darkness falls again
On this elaborate wilderness
And fills the empty minds of men

Where they sit drinking with their wives,
Children asleep but not in bed,
Nothing to atone for but the long,
Blurred perspectives of the dead.

Late Winter Birthday

This broken city, raising a white breath
In the silence, in the first hour of truce,
Gathers the sleepers, their bodies warm and loose
About its shoulders. Asleep on my own path,
These bodies are the start I waken with.
I see my image tottering and the bruise
Of the ageless hour burn and freeze.
My history leaves its crystals in my mouth.

The lamps go out as if they feared the dawn.
Leaning drugged with sleep on the windowsill,
I watch the dawn wind waken the snows
To aimless forage. Somewhere, with measured blows,
A huge black bell is beating what is gone
Into the splintered forest of my will.

The Wandering Jew

When I was a child and thought as a child, I put
The golden prayershawl tassel to my lips
As if I kissed God's hem in my child thought.
I touched the scroll with burning fingertips.

On my left temple there is a shallow dent;
Rabbi called it "the forceps of His will."
I was a boy then, and obedient;
I read the blessings and I read them well.

I strapped my arm and forehead in the faith
With the four thongs of the phylacteries,
Imagining how when we were nearest death,
God brought the proud Egyptians to their knees.

The savage poems, the legends of his mercy
Fell on these years like rain and made them green—
What simple years they were. I loved him fiercely
For loving the Jews and hating the Philistines.

Leaving for evening prayers, I felt the breath
Of the hot street on my face, I saw a door
Alive with shadow, hips and breasts and mouth,
And thought, Is she one? with a thrill of fear.

Filthy scarlet neon. A black drunk
Holding his head together with a rag.
The squad car parked across the street. A bank.
And FUCK YOU chalked on the wall of the synagogue.

One great door took me in, as in a dream.
Rich darkness falling on the congregation,
A voice in the darkness crying Elohim!
And I cried with it, drunk on sweet emotion.

I cannot now remember when I left
That house and its habitual old men
Swaying before the Ark. I was adrift,
And much in need of something I had seen.

At morning and at evening in my head,
A girl in clear silk over nothing on
Smiled with her eyes and all the while her hands
Played with the closing and opening of her gown.

I made the rounds then, married and unmarried,
And either way I seldom slept alone,
But always a familiar presence tarried
Behind the headboard and would not be gone.

Or so I thought. Leaving a girl one night,
I saw how my whole life had been arranged
To meet his anger in a traffic light,
And suddenly I laughed, and the light changed.

And the next night, obedient to my nature,
My head was filled with dew as I leaned to kiss.
Why should I leave this Egypt, while most creatures
Were killing each other in the wilderness?

Sucking for milk and honey at her breasts,
I strained against her till I ground on bone,
And still I heard a whispering of the past
When I awoke beside her in the dawn.

I lay unmoving in the small blue light—
What were the years then but the merest ash
Sprayed by a breath? And what half-buried thought
Fastened its pincers in my naked flesh?

Rabbis, I came, pounding with red knuckles
On the closed Ark, demanding whether a lord
Lived in the vacuum of the Tabernacle
Or had departed, leaving only his word—

3

For years I ate the radish of affliction
Till I was sick of it, and all along
The sparks flew upward, upward. Crucifixion
Screamed at my delicacies of right and wrong.

Blacks swarmed on the stone hills of the city—
Women fucked and abandoned gathered around me—
A sea of voices crying Pity! Pity!
My life's misery rose as if to drown me.

Taste your own bondage in the lives of others—
Isn't it bitter, indigestible food?
If all the wretched of the earth were brothers,
How could I find their father in my god?

I could find rest until a dream of death
Flooded the idling mechanism of my heart:
Nightly now, nomads with broken teeth
Come mumbling brokenly of a black report.

Reeking of gas, they tell what ancient fame,
What mad privation made them what they are,
The dead, the dying—I am one of them—
Dark-blooded aliens pierced with a white star,

A flock of people prey to every horror,
Shattered by thirty centuries of war,
The sport of Christian duke and Hauptsturmfuehrer—
Is this the covenant we were chosen for?

Sometimes, at noon, the dull sun seems to me
A jahrzeit candle for the millions gone
—As if that far, indifferent fire could be
Anything to the black exploded bone!

Tempted and fallen, your Lord God is brooding
Over the ashes where Job sits in pain,
And yet his tribe is ashes, ashes bleeding
And crying out to the sun and to the rain.

I speak of those that lived by rope and spade,
Of those that dug a pit for friend and brother
And later lay down naked in its shade—
There, at last, the prisoners rest together.

I speak it in an anguish of the spirit—
What is man, I ask—what am I?
Am I but one of many to inherit
The barren mountain and the empty sky?

It is a brutal habit of the mind
To look at flesh and tear its clothes away,
It makes consoling speech a figment of wind
And rescue seems like something in a play.

The nights are darker than they used to be.
A squalid ghost has come to share my room
And every night I bring him home with me,
If one can call dissatisfaction home.

All week long I have read in the Pentateuch
Of how I have not lived, and my poor body
Wrestled with every sentence in the book.
If there is Judgment, I will not be ready.

The book I read last night will be my last;
I have come too far lacking a metaphysic.
Live, says the Law—I sit here doing my best,
Relishing meat, listening to music.

Poems from White Blossoms

Et c'est vous et c'est moi. Vous et moi de nouveau, ma vie.
Et je me lève et j'interroge
Les mains d'hôpital de la poussière du matin
Sur les choses que je ne voulais pas revoir.

The End of an Outing

Leaving the pond, she looks like something I know,
hauled-up and dripping, glistening in the sunlight
and swinging her heavy auburn hair she comes to the blanket.

Her eyes are on the trees of the horizon.
I stare at her shoulder and arm,
flushed, and palely freckled, and moist, and cold to the touch.

Behind the pines and cedars the sun is falling,
casting their shadows deep on the empty beach
and the cold red water, suddenly unfamiliar.

In a few minutes, she will undress and sit
alone on the gritty bench of the bathhouse, in semi-dark,
slowly wiping her breasts with a damp towel.

You Could Say

Yesterday rain fell in torrents,
stripping the branches of leaves and
deepening the arroyo. Now,
although the sun glances like flint
at the edges of cars, houses,
antennae, the water remains.
It lies in the hollows of rocks
and in lakes on the roads. Last night
signaled a great change, today
winter breathes at my window and
a few last flies, stunned by cold
into fearlessness, nestle close
to my skin. Summer is burned out.
Why does this season with its joy
in killing and its sweet iron breath
always find me alone? You could say
but you won't, and I am slowly
drifting away, I am growing
oblique like the sun, striking out
feebly at what is gone.

                My love,
it was my nature to want you,
lascivious, aloof, a body
fresh as new-fallen snow, and as
cold. Like other men in my
desire, I asked for it and now
I have it—the wind, the black trees,
scum of ice on the roadside pools—
all that the rain promised, and more.

After Hours

Not yet five, and the light
is going fast. Milky and veined
a thin frost covers the flooded
ruts of the driveway, the grass
bends to the winter night. Her face
is before me now; I see it

in the misted glass, the same
impossible smile and I can feel
again on my bare shoulder
the dew of her breath. We made
a life in two years, a sky
and the very trees, lost in thought.

I know what it is, to be
alone, to have asked for everything
and to do without, to search
the air for a face that dances away,
to wait, and what it exacts.
I don't fear it, I say,

but I do, and this night
the wind against my window
and the top branches thrashing about
enter my life and I see
the coming time loose and dark
above me, with new strength

No Country You Remember

But for the steady wash of rain,
The house is quiet now. Outside,
An occasional car moves past the lawn
And leaves the stillness purified.

I find myself in a dark chair
Idly picking a banjo, lost
In reveries of another time,
Thinking at what heavy cost

I came to this particular place,
This house in which I let my life
Play out its subterranean plot,
My Christian and enduring wife.

What if I paid for what I got?
Nothing can so exhaust the heart
As boredom and self-loathing do,
Which are the poisons of my art.

All day I resurrect the past.
This instrument I love so ill
Hammers and rings and when I wish,
Lies in its coffin and is still.

I dream of winter mornings when
Between bare woods and a wrecked shack
I came down deep encrusted slopes,
A bag of dead birds at my back,

Then let my mind go blank and smile
For what small game the mind demands,
As dead time flickers in the blind
Articulation of my hands.

I know you must despise me, you
Who judge and measure everything
And live by little absolutes—
What would you like to hear me sing?

A strophe on the wasted life?
Some verses dealing with my fall?
Or would you care to contemplate
My contemplation of the wall?

I write from down here, where I live.
In the cold light of a dying day,
The covered page looks cold and dead.
And what more is there to say

Except, you read this in a dream.
I wrote nothing. I sat and ate
Some frozen dinner while I watched
The Late Show, and the Late Late.

The Friendship

What we looked for always remained
in the blue haze drifting behind
our wheels, into the distance.
But our motors roared in concert;
we went into the wind,
faces distended by the wind,
drinking and mouthing in a kind
of brute ecstasy and thirst.
Deafened, with chinese eyes,
we asked what there was to ask
of the onrushing fields, of
the blurred white lines arrowing past
and turned to look at each other,
helmeted, strange, and apart.

2

In the late spring we looked for
snow, and found it in long
rounded patches under the pines.
It was cold in the sunlight
at that height, as we straddled
warm metal and smoked, facing
the timbered slopes where the winter
had come to be. Down below
the river rushed green and white
over the rocks, and a hawk
drifted overhead. Each was there
for the other, and our cheeks burned
in the raw piney darkness
as we raced the downward turns
between big trees, heading home.

3

Tonight the kitchen is warm
and brightly lit and quiet.
I drink his whiskey, he buys

my silence and delicacy.
He drinks and his tongue grows loose.
He loves me up with his lies.
The night cannot end unless
he spills himself, breaks a glass
or falls down, his agony
almost visible, like fumes.
When I reach out to touch him,
there is the empty chair
and the bottle, and he is wheeling
drunkenly down this banked
narrowing space, as if his feet
could say what it is he feels,
or his wet face. I can't speak
or think of what he must want,
and his eyes, behind sungoggles,
turn on me like a blind man's
fervent and terrified—
there is an animal loose
in this house, ripe with the scent
of mania, murderous, bloody, full
of blame, a grown creature
walking at last and beyond his power
to love, pacify, or kill.

Night on Clinton

The bar is closed and I come
to myself outside the door,
drunk and shivering. The talking
champions, the bedroom
killers, the barroom Catholics
have all drifted away and I
am standing in a yellowish
wound of light. Above the blot
my breathing makes on the glass,
I look down the darkened bar
where the bottles are out of breath,
the stale tumblers bunched, and white
glistening webs in the pitchers
dry up and shrivel.
The plastic stools turn
in the hot light that bubbles
from the big Sea Bird, silent now,
and a shape vaguely human
moves with a rag and a limp
among the tables
piled high with surrendered chairs.
Nailed on the back wall, a great
Canadian elk fixes me
with his glazed liquid eyes and
the last lights go out. What I see
is important now, but I see
only the dim half-moon
of my own face in the black
mirror of space, and I lay
my cheek against the cold glass.
Snow is beginning to fall,
huge wet flakes that burst from
the darkness like parachutes
and plunge past the streaming light
and melt into the street.
Freeze, die, says the veteran wind

from the north but he goes on
with his work, the night and the snow,
and was not speaking to me.

The Next Thing is Always About to Happen

A letter arrives, *We hope to arrive tomorrow,*
can you meet us in King of Prussia?
Or, *I owe too much money.* Always the new
word like the old action carried into someone's hands.

And he is reminded suddenly of his life.
It is late morning, cool and limpid,
the breezes damp with honeysuckle. *Six months now*
and I still can't remember she's not in the house alive.

So many lives are like pages I read in a book,
but the pages are torn and lost. Life goes on.
A bus exhales in the echoing terminal,
a face swims to the glass from the dark interior.

In the middle of sleep where they are forbidden to enter,
the threads are trembling, the garbled message
burns on the wind: *our city in flames, in ruins,*
and the dead are straggling home with their red brows.

Whatever I think of is fingers that stretch toward me,
thin bones in a filthy envelope of flesh,
and I am a strong man, as strength goes,
with weakness swelling in every joint and gesture.

Our need reaches stubbornly down with a chancellor's hand
and we are equally gripped. Day after day
there is silence in King of Prussia
and thin black plumes of smoke hanging over the land.

Back

Tonight I looked at the pale northern sky
Above the city lights, and both the stars
And the lamps of men faded and burned by turns,
Breathed in and out. You would have liked it here,
The emptiness, the wind across the fields,
And the spring coming on—especially
The strange white almond blossoms, their unfolding
When a car swings down the lane towards the orchard
And turns its headlights on them. Hard as it was,
I forced myself to think of everything
You liked best, the years before you died
In a locked room in an Army hospital.
Or was it after that, in a Southern city,
Watching the traffic lights go on and off
And the big-finned cars swim past in a blur of rain?
I know your heart stopped once when, slightly drunk,
Holding your daughter's hand, you stood before
The cage of a small, shuddering European bear.
That spring in Half Moon Bay, where the sad surf
Felt up and down the beach with endless sighs,
And in the morning the brown seaweed lay
Like old surgical tubing. It could have been
Any one of a hundred times and places.
But last night, opening my eyes from sleep
To the steady courtyard light, I heard your breath
Coming and going like a wounded thing
That would not die. It could have been
Nothing but mine, persisting one more night.

There

It is deep summer. Far out
at sea, the young squalls darken
and roll, plunging northward,
threatening everything. I see
the Atlantic moving in slow
contemplative fury
against the rocks, the beaten
headlands, and the towns sunk deep
in a blind northern light. Here,
far inland, in the mountains
of Mexico, it is raining
hard, battering the soft mouths
of flowers. I am sullen, dumb,
ungovernable. I taste myself
and I taste those winds, uprisings
of salt and ice, of great trees
brought down, of houses and cries
lost in the storm; and what breaks
on that black shore breaks in me.

Looking

There are brown weeds bent down hard in the steady blow
And mustard and winterberry, magnified, bright in the wet,
There are fields blurred away to a slowly dissolving horizon
As I drive on the glassy black road, going home.
Draped on the wheel, I stare at the three days' rain
And dim scattered lights drowning out in the early darkness
Of houses huddled patiently under their elms.
But tomorrow morning, a light sharpened on glaciers
Will stream from the sky between exhausted low clouds,
And the mountains eighty miles away will have moved
Close on the flat suburbs and grown wrinkled.
And all of this, the storming, the raw peaks
In the massive wheel of light, these are new signs—
I believe them as they would be believed.
In the rooms I come to, touched by so many hands
And tasted by other rains, I stand at the door
And learn how a chair endures its wearing away,
The dustballs at its feet, the dead lamp
Arching above it like a stuffed giraffe.
There is a table, there is the black stove,
And somewhere a clock is beating.
                                        This is life,
The curls of blood clouding the toiletbowl,
Bound for darkness; and the crooked lines
The rain makes on the windows; and not least,
These hazel haunted eyes, this livid mouth
Buried up to the lips in drifts of white—
Day after day, this strange face in the mirror
Which I awkwardly shave and study with shy glimpses;
And all the while, the flaking roads and clouds,
The rain, the mountains, the weeds, and the cool light
That bathes it all, even the lamps and chairs,
Are building a life more formidable than our own
Of what is true about them, which they know
By not knowing, going unnoticed, and looking.

The doe standing poised

The doe standing poised
in the deep rut
ribbed with shadows
of larch and pine

the brown eye
brimming with sunlight
among the leaves
turned and was gone

The spade that was plunged
into the earth this morning
leans facing its shadow
on the white fence

Coming Home

I have been waiting a long time.

The door is open,
The lamp shines on the oilcloth,
The old man's face hidden in light
Asleep.

A Confession

If someone was walking across
your lawn last night, it was me.
While you dreamt of prowlers, I was
prowling down empty lanes, to breathe
the conifer coolness of just
before dawn. Your flowers were closed,
your windows black and withdrawn.

Sometimes I see a square of
yellow light shining through the trees,
and I cross the grass and look in.
Your great body on the bed
is nude and white, and though I'm starved
for love like everyone, the sight
of your black sex leaves me cold.

What would I say to a squad car
if it came on its noiseless tires
and picked me out with its lights, like
a cat or a rabbit? That I
only wanted to see how people
live, not knowing how? That I
haven't had a woman in months?

Therefore I stay out of sight
and do not speak. Or if I speak,
I make small animal sounds
to myself, so as not to wake you.
And I touch myself. What
I wanted to do was enter
and bend and touch you on the cheek.

My Mother

My mother writes from Trenton,
a comedian to the bone
but underneath serious
and all heart. 'Honey,' she says,
'be a mensch and Mary too,
its no good, to worry, you
are doing the best you can
your Dad and everyone
thinks you turned out very well
as long as you pay your bills
nobody can say a word
you can tell them, to drop dead
so save a dollar it can't
hurt—remember Frank you went
to highschool with? he still lives
with his wife's mother, his wife
works while he writes his books and
did he ever sell a one
the four kids run around naked
36, and he's never had,
you'll forgive my expression
even a pot to piss in
or a window to throw it,
such a smart boy he couldnt
read the footprints on the wall
honey you think you know all
the answers you dont, please, try
to put some money away
believe me it wouldn't hurt
artist shmartist life's too short
for that kind of, forgive me,
horseshit, I know what you want
better than you, all that counts
is to make a good living
and the best of everything,
as Sholem Aleichem said,
he was a great writer did
you ever read his books dear,

you should make what he makes a year
anyway he says some place
Poverty is no disgrace
but its no honor either
that's what I say,
                    love,
                        Mother'

Touch It

Out on the bare grey roads
I pass by vineyards withering toward winter,
cold magenta shapes and green fingers,
the leaves rippling in the early darkness.
Past the thinning orchard the fields
are on fire. A mountain of smoke
climbs the desolate wind, and at its roots
fire is eating dead grass with many small teeth.
When I get home, the evening sun
has narrowed to a filament. When it goes
and the dark falls like a hand on a tabletop,
I am told that what we love most is dying.
The coldness of it is even on this page
at the edge of your fingernail. Touch it.

The Underground Gardens

for Baldasare Forestiere

Sick of the day's heat, of noise
and light and people, I come
to walk in Forestiere's
deep home, where his love never
came to live; where he prayed to Christ;
slept lightly; put on his clothes;
clawed at the earth forty years
but it answered nothing.
Silence came down with the small
pale sunlight, then the darkness.
Maybe the girl was dead. He
grew accustomed to the silence
and to the darkness. He brought
food to his mouth with both
invisible hands, and waited
for night's darkness to give way
to the darkness of day. If
he held his breath and his
eyes closed against the brown light
sifting down by masonry and roots,
he could see her spirit among
his stone tables, laughing and
saying no. When he opened
them to emptiness, he wept.
And at last he kept them closed.
Death gripped him by the hair and
he was ready. He turned and slept
more deeply.

          There were many
rooms, tunnels and coves and arbors,
places where men and women
could sit, flowering plazas
where they could walk or take food,
and rooms for the tired to rest.

He could almost imagine
their voices, but not just yet.

He is buried somewhere else.

Reaching the Horizon

Once it was enough simply
to be here. Neither to know
nor to be known, I crossed
in the full sight of everything
that stood dumbly in sunlight
or drank the standing water
when it was clear. I called them
by their names and they were what
I called them. In the low glare
of afternoon I advanced
upon my shadow, glancing
at the grass unoccupied,
into the wind and into
the light. What I did not know
passed shuddering toward me
over the bowed tips of the
grass and what I could not see
raced sunward away from me
like dust crystals or a wave
returning to its yellow source.

This morning the wet black eye
of a heifer darkens with the
passing seconds, holding my gaze.
It has grown cold. Flies
drop from the wall; guinea fowl
roost in the sycamore. Old
dog in the corner, the day
ripples into its fullness.
Surrounded by eyes and tongues,
I begin to feel the waste
of being human. The rose
of the sky darkens to a wound
and closes with one question
on its lips, and the million
stars rise up into the blackness
with theirs. If I spoke to this

formerly it was as one
speaks to a mirror or scummed
pond, not guessing how deep it is—
Now I see what has no name
or singularity and
can think of nothing to say.

To Her

Risen above the uncertain
boughs in the last breath of daylight,
so near she seems that you can
touch her with your hand, she rides
in the tall blue silence.
Her light falls across the fields
like drifted snow. The shadow
of the pale barn is like something
alive, softer than fur.
                            No one
acknowledges what is happening,
it has happened so many times
and it means nothing. The city
lights vault against the night sky
far off and headlights enter
and leave the dark. All have their own
or other lights to follow,
all have their place.
                            Only a dog
gives tongue in this outer dark,
and the insect nations keep
their high-pitched vigil. The gaunt
illiterate sheriff, scratching his nose,
looks upward and is reminded
of other nights, things done
by hands and knives, the flesh laid open,
flashed under shirt or dress
and the young boy and girl give up
their first nakedness to her
as they struggle with their mouths
to come together. Things fight and sleep.
And this one, stumbling alone
in a thicket of wishes, feeling
the new bristles on his face,
confesses her power from his knees.

How else can he explain
the inexplicable? When he drove

a thousand miles without rest,
when he pleaded with his girl, when
he ran away, broke his hand, went down
on someone's wife, drank and was sick,
stole money, walked in the woods,
came here to change—if he dare
make his voice heard in this
luminous darkness, who is there
to hear? Only the full moon,
and to her all sounds are music.

White Blossoms

Take me as I drive alone
through the dark countryside.
As the strong beams clear a path,
picking out fences, weeds, late
flowering trees, everything
that streams back into the past
without sound, I smell the grass
and the rich chemical sleep
of the fields. An open moon
sails above, and a stalk
of red lights blinks, miles away.

It is at such moments I
am called, in a voice so pure
I have to close my eyes and enter
the breathing darkness just beyond
my headlights. I have come back,
I think, to something I had
almost forgotten, a mouth
that waits patiently, sighs, speaks
and falls silent. No one else
is alive. The blossoms are
white, and I am almost there.

The Mercy of Sorrow

Ten Poems from Uri Zvi Greenberg

The Hour

The hour is very weary, as before sleep.
Like a foundling child, just in my white shirt,
I sit and write in space, as on a slate—
    No matter, no matter.

Should the black cat come to the pitcher and lick
The remnants of milk and overturn the pitcher,
I will close my eyes to sleep, and sleep forever—
    No matter, no matter.

Joy

And what is joy? A going up
So as to come down harder,
Hurtling into anguish?

Yes, there's a bridge from sorrow to sorrow.
In the middle a bush bursts into flames,
A heat that dries up the tear
Gathering on the eyelash—

Until the rejoicer reaches
Across, to the other side.

With my God, the Smith

Like chapters of prophecy my days burn, in all the revelations,
And my body between them's a block of metal for smelting,
And over me stands my God the Smith, who hits hard:
The wounds that Time has opened in me, open their mouths
                                        to him
And release in a shower of sparks the intrinsic fire.

This is my just lot—until dusk on the road.
And when I return to throw my beaten block on a bed,
My mouth is an open wound
And naked I speak with my God:
                        You worked hard.
Now it is night, come, let us both rest.

Like a Girl

Like a girl who knows that her body drives me to begging,
God taunts me, Flee if you can! But I can't flee,
For when I turn away from him, angry and heartsick,
With a vowel on my lips like a burning coal:
I will not see him again—

I can't do it.
And I turn back
And knock on his door,
Tortured with longing

As though he had sent me a love-letter.

The Great Sad One

The Almighty has dealt bitterly with me
That I did not believe in him until my punishment,
Till he welled up in my tears, from the midst of my wounds.
And behold—he also is very lonely,
And he also lacks someone to confess to,
In whose arms he might sob his unbearable misery.

And this God walks about, without a body, without blood,
And his grief is double the grief of flesh,
Flesh that can warm another body or a third,
That can sit and smoke a cigarette,
And drink coffee and wine,
And sleep and dream until the sun—

For him, it is impossible, for he is God.

On the Equator

How rarely your mercy visits me,
My king, my father;
And so, most of my days, I am your wandering son
Who has cast his lot like a prophet
In the desert of his days.

And your deliverance that comes to me then,
My father, my king,
Is like a well that the wanderer came on at last,
When he had almost prayed for death from thirst
And the heat that shrivels the body.

And at times it is so sweet,
It is like a miraculous dream that you give
To the blind man in his agony, at night.
He dreams that his eyes are open and that he sees
The face of his wife and the dark gold of her hair.

But at times you make sport of me,
My father, my king, and I draw back
And grow small with loneliness, like the blind man awakened
                                                    from his dream.
I gaze at my coming days, and I descend
Into the black abyss of my life, as the blind man into his.

There is a Box

There is a box and a coverlet, and a pair of black horses
Stepping forth heavily, in honor, of course, of the grief.
There is a spade, and a strong man, the digger,
White linen, and a girl who sews.

Adam is dust, the Rabbi must surely be rotting by now,
And what remains in writing—a doctrine of no death.
I speak of what feeds down there in the mire!
There is nothing in books, only a few words.

How It Is

I hear the sound of affliction. They are weeping,
It seems—human beings, male and female.
Once I heard only the joy of those who were married
To the juice and sweetness of life.

There's no need to ask why they weep—it's clear enough.
If women are weeping, it's a sign of their defilement;
If men, what could it mean but the loss
Of great faiths as powerful as the earth?

Souls that go forth gaily on their wanderings,
Adorned with their colorful visions,
How wan they are, and shrunken, when they come back!

The Valley of Men

I have never been on the cloudy slopes of Olympus.
In the living man's valley I grew with the bread.
Like other men, I drank the sweet water there,
Waters where cattle drank, whose flesh I ate.

The Queen's train my forefathers did not carry, amongst the
                                                  Gentiles.
The King did not call them, either in sorrow or in joy.
They were poor Jews, shining and singing,
Little more than the shepherd blows through his flute.

So I am pleased to carry myself from sorrow to sorrow,
As the shepherd his littlest sheep from pasture to pasture,
And he eats a few figs, to keep the breath in his body—

Red seamed are the ends of my days and nights.

On the Pole

Some clouds are rainclouds—
On my head like a mist the mercy of sorrow transpires.
It is good to command the boat of all longings:
Stop and anchor.

For here is the Pole—and joy is native
To the country of youth, garlanded with beauty.
It is good to descend, to rake in the remnants of honey
And the white milk—in the final place.

The Door Standing Open

*I am putting my words together for whatever
Intelligence there may be in the world. There
is no other reality among men than this
intelligence.... To be more than I thought I was—
a sensation utterly new to me ...*

*That power we had felt flowing in us and through
us could not, in the nature of things, be acutely
conscious of us as individuals. It must come
rather as wind comes to the trees of a forest, or
as the ocean continues to murmur in the seashell
it has thrown ashore.*

E

At the Point

Travelers long on the road
stop here for water and for the view.
Their children run
through the young and old pines,
splashing in the needles
or chasing the wild canaries, their
light cries
receding in the aisles of shade.

The light is so simple
and steady,
as if tiny beaks
had opened a vein of pure sunlight in the forest,
and the fathers and mothers
stand looking down,
their lives
jumping at the base of their throats
and little words
unspoken for twenty or thirty years
cling to their lips like droplets of water.

In the valley the taut fences
stretch pitilessly to the horizon
and all those who want to be someplace else
must follow them.
The hawks and owls crucified on the wire
have long since returned to their own country,
and the mouse trembles in ecstasy,
lost in the shadow of their wings.

How Much Longer?

Day after day after day it goes on
and no one knows how to stop it or escape.
Friends come bearing impersonal agonies,
I hear our hopeless laughter, I watch us drink.
War is in everyone's eyes, war is made
in the kitchen, in the bedroom, in the car at stoplights.
A marriage collapses like a burning house
and the other houses smolder. Old friends
make their way in silence. Students stare
at their teachers, and suddenly feel afraid.
The old people are terrified like cattle
rolling their eyes and bellowing, while the young
wander in darkness, dazed, half-believing
some half-forgotten poem, or else come out
with their hearts on fire, alive in the last days.
Small children roam the neighborhoods armed
with submachineguns, gas masks and riot sticks.
Excavations are made in us and slowly
we are filled in with used-up things: knives
too dull to cut bread with, bombs that failed to go off,
cats smashed on the highway, broken pencils,
slivers of soap, hair, gristle, old TV sets
that hum and stare out blindly like the insane.
Bridges kneel down, the cities billow and plunge
like horses in their smoke, the tall buildings
open their hysterical burning eyes at night,
the leafy suburbs look up at the clouds and tremble—

and my wife leaves her bed before dawn, walking
the icy pasture, shrieking her grief to the cows,
praying in tears to the softening blackness. I hear her
outside the window, crazed, inconsolable,
and go out to fetch her. Yesterday she saw
a photograph, Naomi our little girl
in a ditch in Viet Nam, half in the water,
the rest of her, beached on the mud, was horribly burned.

Theresienstadt Poem

In your watercolor, Nely Sílvinová
your heart on fire
on the grey cover of a sketchbook
is a dying sun or
a flower
youngest of the summer

the sun itself
the grizzled head of a flower
throbbing
in the cold dusk of your last day
on earth

There are no thorns to be seen
but the color says
thorns

and much else that is not
visible it says also
a burning wound at the horizon
it says Poland and winter
it says painful Terezín
SILVIN VI 25 VI 1944
and somehow
above the light body on its bed of coals
it says spring
from the crest of the street it says
you can see the fields
brown and green
and beyond them the dark blue line of woods
and beyond that smoke
is that the smoke of Prague
and it says blood
every kind of blood
blood of Jews
German blood
blood of Bohemia and Moravia

running in the gutters
blood of children
it says free at last
the mouth of the womb it says
SILVIN VI 25 VI 1944
the penis of the commandant
the enraged color
the whip stock the gun butt
it says it says it says

Petrified god
god that gave up the ghost at Terezín
what does it say but itself
thirteen years of life
and your heart on fire
                    Nely Sílvinová!

Nocturne

The nightfall is endless
for the children
cowering in dancehalls
or on the high peaks condemned to break eagles

The laboring men
with their simple scars and elaborate paintings
stand transfixed
by the last ray of sun on the white
factory wall

Some sit beside those praying for courage
to bandage the filthiest head
but many more kneel
when the voice of the prophet
echoes in the pewter mugs of the rich

This is where you come in
where you are taken to the cashiers
cage in the hall of mirrors
where you hurl your delicate feelings
at a face as thick as a thigh
in a numbered tongue
and this is where you leave

Over the ranch house roof
the smoke of piety
curls a forelock round one finger
and the stovepipe
the stovepipe is about to take wing
its black warhead giving suck
to the pale starlight

Nolan

Who will come leading a horse,
a gentle horse with the eyes
of a good mother,
who will lead it to Nolan
who is barely five years old?
Nolan leaps on the back
of a barren mare
whose eyes, though they brim with sorrow,
are painted eyes
(and Nolan's are always the same,
empty, emptier than hunger)
and pressing his small groin
to the stiff scrolled mane
he rides,
and the mare bucks wildly in her frame.
All day and all night he rides,
but if he had a sword,
a real sword and not too big
for such a little boy,
he would drive it into her side
where the hollow entrails are,
and saw at the ragged lips
till he reached the heart
that has never learned to beat,
and his eyes filled with tears
and his bones with cold fire
and his mouth with the one word,
mama mama mama
falling on deaf ears.

To Gary, at the Threshold of the House

1

Again the rain thundering on the tin roof
an avalanche of pebbles,
rain fallen for weeks and weeks
the drowned fields can't hold any more.
Thousands of little rivers
run through the woods up here,
plucking old strings, making
new grass. Soon it will be the time
of the blue-eyed grass,
the time of the redbud and the red maid.
Already the crimson head
of the snow plant, a hard cock
butts through the membrane, pushes aside
black crumbs of earth, breaking
into light.
On the shoulders of cow trails
the dead turn over again.
Wherever you go,
your son is yawning in Anna's belly.

2

Hard to believe they could want you now,
that swamped, listing table load
of red-wattled judges, cadaverous undertakers,
tight car dealers, doctors, well-to-do butchers spouting
that incomprehensible bad poetry,
running down ghostly corridors in their glad rags
flapping like the freaky echoes of a bad trip,
crying all night
        'Gary, it's time
to plant your bloodflowers in the hump of Asia'
and other wild things
that make you laugh.

I see them walking round
and round
where you sit naked, lotus
slowly dissolving
in unearthly smiles, unmoving
bringing
everything to bear on the instant
of birth.

3

What can they take away?
Your fancy wide belt from St. Vincent de Paul's?
A pinch of Panama Red, poem books, shoelace,
your cowboy shirt, your golden hair,
your big home-made mandala?
They can take you from this prison
and put you in that prison
and say
      'It's time to suffer now, Gary'
and swing locked the heavy echoing doors
and walk away,
leaving you all your possessions. . .

4

wildflowers
on wet breasts, silken threads
the silence buzzing
unceasing after-vibration of some great bass string
a sound you were waiting for,
the stars caught
in a net of twigs, glimmering
in the darkest
meat of your brain—
and you're already halfway through the door
and away, the door
standing open.

California Farewell

Tonight,
in a torn shirt,
in the last of the daylight
I leave the road
to its distances, dove
that flies away into the sky.

I still see your car
getting small,
fatalist metal rolling, rolling
to the dark beat of poles,
fence posts,
that blurred strip which was the desert—
your eyes fixed
on the endlessly receding vision.

Why are you leaving me?
I feel
like a raw baby in my open red shirt.

2

I see the sun
give up everything without a struggle,
burning itself
into that powerful line that has no memory,
horizon
dancing away in radiant acid.

Something is sleeping
just beneath the poor grains of the earth,
ear pressed to the silence.

Now
I can say goodbye,
in the privacy of the twilight,
in the darkness closing around me,
the petals of darkness
closing up for the night.

A Prayer in His Sickness

You brought me, lord,
to these sun-punished hills,
this Academy
where I opened my eyes and my ears
to the peacock braying
and the peahen running over the fields,
where I bent to the grass my brother
sleepy and red at the close of the day
and made my farewells.
You brought me, lord.

You bring me now
to the mouth of my 33rd year
but I'm afraid to drink
of this black water.
Weak hands, weak heart,
liverish spittle, lips
shaped and bled dry by so many cravings,
my whole life at sundown dissolving into the grass—
I turn away,
and you turn away in despair.

Be with me now.
Don't let me speak with my painted tongue
to the ghosts of this world.
Let me put off
this heavy finery, let me put off my suffering flesh
and I will come down to meet you, lord,
wherever you say.

Going for a Walk at Night

It is very late.
Few stars are left and those blinking
Like the eyes of a sleepy child.

I feel with my hand
Under the ribs of the wind
But I can't tell anything,
I feel with my foot in the dust
But all I touch
Is the few green tongues of the dead.

Looking back to where I started
I see
A door of golden light
Opening in the roots of the dark trees.
There sleep
The children who are not mine,
The wife who is not mine
And my life.

The road is only a darkness
Between darker banks,
Weeds that turn in their sleep
And pillars
That go whistling off into the void.

Unmoving
In the autumn cold,
I stand a long time
Until time flickers
And goes out in a pool of darkness.
Smoke rises from my lungs
And disappears
Among the last stars.

Going to Heaven

She went on her knees in the dirt
thinking of nothing
lost in the crumbling blackness
kneeling above her shadow
preparing
a place for bulbs
and a few seeds held in the palm of her hand.

Now gladiolus rises everywhere
perfect in sunlight
spreading straight green wings into the air
and green curls in the shade
that will be eaten.

And I have dug
steps in the dark earth
that we may descend to them.

Pisces' Car Song

All night driving south
I carried your pure mountain water,
hearing it slosh in the invisible glass
in the darkness behind me, following
lights down the flowery tunnels of the night
and rolled past first pink derricks of San Diego
heading into the desert
toward the slowly kindling skull of Sierra San Pedro Martir.

When the sun burst up in flames
I saw it
lightly chopping in the clear 5 gallon jug,
swaying past
cracked gullies round Yuma, the unliftable dead stones
of the Territorial Prison,
past black wings rising heavily on Highway 80
and a lone ragged black man
wilderness walker,
little puffs of dust pursuing his shoes—
north of Live Oak Springs I saw two white-faced steers
ambling in sage and long sunrise shadows
and remembered myself,
the dark face streaked with sweat—
among 10,000 acres.

Between Santa Ana and Hermosillo
I stopped on the side of the road, unstopped the jug
and put my mouth to its mouth.
It was like drinking of you,
nearer than my breastbone and yet so far.

I hope you meet me Tuesday,
I have your pure mountain water.

There Goes Gatten

There goes a man on a long journey
Hurrying toward the almost religious solitude
Of the middle of the night.
Many nights he sat
At the open window listening
Sadly to the shrill of the small insects

Grinding their prayer machines in the grass
And great branches bending endlessly
To the breath that visits only a moment
The mouths of the living—
Endlessly, and he covered his face with his hands.
Now it is time to go on.

Poem

I am looking for someone to speak in this poem
Someone not I
Who can say
I without blushing
With a veiled smile

The other voices all belong to me now
And I can't remember where I borrowed them

If you have something to give
Give it to the man who vanishes into the rock
To the one who watches and speaks
Behind his mask
Without breaking into giggles

As for myself I mistrust
My name my face
My fourth eye
The shadow of my hands in which
Ants scurry to their deaths

I predict my own death
When all my poems will fly back into my mouth

Small crystals
Dissolving in the acid of truth

New Year's Eve in Solitude

Night comes to the man who can pray
only on paper.
He disappears into paper
with his old mouth shaped to say no
and his voice is so tiny
in all these miles of silence and cold grass.

As I write
the fog has eaten away the mountains
the princely hills and the fields
everything but this house
and this hand
and the few feet of light it throws out against the dark.

I try to talk
to the drunken god who sleeps in my arms and legs
tell him god knows what
but what's the use he won't listen
or else he listens in his sleep

and the dead listen in theirs
up on the hill
up past the drifting
iron gates the dead leaves
listen and the frozen
water pipes.

And at last I know what to ask.
I know what I really want
and it hurts me.

Nothing any more against the darkness,
nothing against the night,
nothing
in which the bright child is silent and shines very dimly,
cover me with your arms,
give me your breast,
that will make me forgetful and slow
so I can join him in sleep—

Hurry down now good mother, give me
my life again
in this hand that lives but a moment and is immortal,
cover my eyes and I will see them,
those companions clothed head to foot in tiny fires
that I said goodbye to when I first opened my eyes.

Give me my robes of earth
and my black milk

April Fourth

I throw open the door
And someone like the night walks in

A moist wind in the doorway
A breath of flowers
In the wake of this august presence

I was sitting for hours
Watching the coal
Of the cigarette rising and falling
Finally one must do something

The evening I thought
The evening was the last evening
As usual

I was thinking of heroes
Whose knuckles shine as they curl round a rifle
I was thinking of my brother
Who brings me my head in a basket
What is there to do

Let me make myself empty
I can live without sleeping tonight

I can live without dreams of the King
Awash on his balcony
Half of his neck and face in another kingdom

In the morning I will not understand

Mountains surfacing from their mortal darkness
A scum of yellow flowers
The great oak crying with a thousand voices

All that
Wrinkles like heat and disappears into thin air

Lines Written in Terror

Was it only a dream
The city trying to retch
Smell of blood
Blackness spreading from the mouth down
Gagged sounds
Wake me thrashing and burning
In the wet graveclothes

I prayed I would find
The least blue light on the bed
But outside it's still dark so much for prayer

At this hour they are on the streets
Running down
Everything caught in their lights
Retarded stoned
Nocturnal makers of songs
Painters of poems still dripping from brick walls
And they are working fast
In the blackness their gloves flash
Opening eyes and lips
Of poor fools who said something or
Looked at them funny
And what they did to a girl

I tell you
There are things that must not be said
Hearing them
Men want to die
Men want to kill

Kaleidoscope

Everywhere man is born free
And everywhere he is in chains
I remember reading that
And laugh bitterly but we are no different

Ideas surround me with spears
And certain images
Climb up before dawn and bang at the silence
Instruments of torture

Black wings converging on all the roads
A sudden flash of teeth deep in the sea
And there is a glass tear shining
On the helmets of the police

My sight descends into the blackness
That begins at the muzzle and gets deeper
No end no end to the blackness
Of that implacable hole

The flag of my country
Freshly laundered whips in the breeze
It is a beautiful morning
A man is beaten to death under the County Jail

I have been up all night
Toying with words
And hiding my face in my hands
I walked outside

The stars set so slowly
In a few minutes they were gone
And there was nothing nothing at all
In the pale blue sky

One Summer

My father coming home
from the factory
summer and still light out
the green bus at the end
of the endless street
the foul sigh
on which my father stepped down
walking slowly in the shadows
holding my hand
my father tired and frowning
eating his supper of potatoes
reading the Bulletin
news of the war
and columns of boxscores
my father singing lewd hymns
in his tuneless voice
stretched out full length in the tub
his calves hanging over the rim
his long penis resting
on the surface of the grey water

Last Words

To John Lawrence Simpson 1897–1969

Like men who meet
for the first time from opposite ends of the earth,
we never talked much.
You sat
at the kitchen table, in a chair
only the smallest children dared to sit in,
yelling at your sons or telling some sly story,
or silent, looking out the window,
and I sat next to you
with my hands folded,
staring at your daughter, barely listening,
a writer of books, a poet.

Now what was faithful
most of a century to the earth
and the darkness of earth
is preparing to become the earth,
and what was faithful to the light
is turning painfully into light.
Now I want to say
what I have never said.

Old man, sometimes I felt like a child
sitting next to you.
I watched your hands
that were strong and twisted as if pulled from the earth
and the blue smoke curling upward in the silence
and felt like a child.

There were many things I did not understand.
How easily fooled I was
by your fierceness, your long silences,
your rants against communism.
How easily I assumed
your distaste for my long hair and my long face
and my long history of childhood.
Still, I listened to your stories

and I remember well
the mules straining in the darkness, the bitter thin air,
the mountain road covered with snow, the huge logs
covered with snow,
and summer nights in the old days,
wild girls riding bareback over the foothills,
sisters of rustlers, going to a dance,
and the old Harley
hitting a big hole and going down thrashing and burning
in the gravel,
and I remember what I saw,
long after midnight in the cold shed,
the long rip in the cow's side,
the silent man with his arm
plunged in up to his shoulder, the cow's head
secured in the iron stanchions, her eyes
black and enormous with agony,
the cloud of her breath, the cloud of mine,
no sound, blood everywhere,
I remember what I saw in your eyes.

And I see
drifting through the smoke and fog
the cool sun—
through the wreckage of years, cars,
dead pigeons, dead wives,
good deals and foolish charity,
money made and lost,
made again and lost again,
a dead baby, a dead son growing rich in the east,
the leaves dying on the vine,
the dying sun,
through death and divorce and dull disaster,
a young and tender spirit.

The road is paved,
the hole filled in,

the girls lie under the stones
of Academy Cemetery
many years.
All the old mountain men
gone for good into the mountains,
the sound of their laughter growing very faint,
and the wind keeps blowing.

In the Soul Hour

Tonight I could die as easily as the grass
and I can't help thinking
whenever the light flickers along the finished blood red boards
how just the other side
of the fiery grain
the skull of the house is clapped in darkness

The joys of our lives tonight
the dance sweat the shining sidelong eyes
the faint sweet cuntsmells hiding in perfume

music from another planet

voices at night
carried across the blowing water

I Am Here

For Naomi, later

I want to speak to you while I can,
in your fourth year before you can well understand,
before this river
white and remorseless carries me away.

You asked me to tell you about death.
I said nothing. I said

This is your father,
this is your father like water,
like fate,
like a feather circling down.

And I am my own daughter
swimming out,
a phosphorescence on the dark face of the surf.

A boat circling on the darkness.

2

She opens her eyes under water. The sun climbs.
She runs, she decapitates flowers.
The grass sparkles. Her little brother laughs.
She serves meals to friends no one has seen.
She races her tricycle in circles.
I come home. The sun falls.

3

You eat all day.
You want to be big. 'Look how big!'
you cry,
stretching your arms to heaven,
your eyes stretched
by all the half terrified joy of being in motion.

The big move clumsily, little love,
as far as I can see.

They break everything
and then they break,
and a pool of decayed light sinks back into the earth.

Writing these words tonight,
I am coming to the end
of my 35th year. It means nothing to you,
but I rejoice and I am terrified
and I feel something I can never describe.
They are so much the same,
so much the sun blazing on the edge of a knife. . . .

We are little children
and my face has already entered the mist.

4

I hear you cry out
in the blackened theatre of night.
I go in and hold you in my arms
and rock you, watching
your lips working,
your closed eyelids bulge with the nightly vision.

5

I get lost too, Naomi,
in a forest that suddenly rises
from behind my breastbone on a night of no moon.
Stars hang in the black branches,
great, small,
glittering like insoluble crimes,
ceaselessly calling me
toward that thick darkness under the trees.
I turn, sobbing, to run,
but it is everywhere.

6

I wanted to give you something
but always give you something else.

What do you call it when it is underground
like a cold spring in the blood,
when it is a poem written out of naked fear
and love which is never enough,
when it is my face, Naomi,
my face
from which the darkness streams forth?

The petal falls,
the skin crumbles into dirt,
consciousness likewise crumbles
and this is one road the squirrel will not cross again.

I was here, Naomi,

I will never be back
but I was here,
I was here with you and your brother.

In This Life

Now the cup of grasses and down is cool,
the eggs cool, the throne empty
from which she would step down and growing still,
look out long toward the darkness.

One moist and terrible night, it came creeping
and tensing its jaws and it too grew still
and then it had her,
and a small diamond of light opened in her brain.

I remember the eyes closed tight
against the final ecstasy of the teeth,
the weightless blood-beaded lump of feathers buried now
under the iris slowly eaten alive by the air.

Here is the father
blossoming on a twig
to sing the song of the bleeding throat
on this day of crystal wind and young sunlight.

He sings the endless song
of irises wrinkling and wrinkling and becoming nothing,
road of fine sand strewn with fallen wings,
the mouse, the toad, the blind nestling taken in deep grass,

he sings of a diamond, sings
of the spokes flashing brilliance at the center
of the ceaselessly collapsing floor of bone
and I wish I sang with him,

he sings the only truth
in this world where men remember mostly lies,
sings it and sings it
till it breaks at last into particles of light,

blossoms of mercy
in the midst of the holocaust.

An Evening

The sun blazing slowly in its last hour

A horse motionless on a knoll
His long neck and mouth plunged toward the earth
His tail blowing in filaments of fire

Tuft of grass that bends its illuminated head over its own shadow
The grass sleepy after the long feast of light

And the new leafed figs dancing a little in the silence
Readying themselves for the night

An evening

Understood
By those who understand it not

Watching the Invisible

wind climbing swiftly the steep hillside
the grass rearing and plunging like the ocean

day of wind day of barely
audible music driving the seed heads crazy
thin bodies twisted and swaying and bent down flat

wind printed with fossils and jewels
wind uttering flashes of light
revelation visiting everything the same
the wind brushing my bare skin with its silk like a girl
going in and out of flesh as through a door—

When I climb dripping out of the old frog pond
wind is there to meet me
certain cold
thoughts racing ahead of the sunlight
not of death . . .

no, but I think of the day sinking back into darkness
and the hands held up dripping with it
the hands held up
drying themselves in the wind

Song

Stars overhead
A frog's grunt from the other side of the pond
Clear sound in the summer night

Ollie is asleep
My warm foxy girls
Curled up at my sides
In my lap the story of a king and his youngest daughter

The perfume of hair
Little Omi is breathing the pure breath of sleep

Eve moves to the open door
My senses are full
Of her slim young womanly body
And tinkling anklets

I am ready for sleep

Orion blows like a kite in the summer sky
I think I will climb up his tail
To freedom

I am Beginning to Hear

a voice in this life I am living
every day every night
never before heard

speaking in languages
made of shifts in the direction of the wind
seeds fallen from an apple

there is a flight of arrows or is it light
turning the way things turn
after the sun
only at different speeds

brilliant darkness as in the night when there is no moon
I must have known it once

as now
moving easily as a hand
among the fiery lights raining out of space
I know what is said but it is
dark untranslatable

a flower suddenly folding up
and rushing away into its ancient parchments